THE CATECHISM
OF THE CATHOLIC CHURCH
ON

LITURGY

AND

SACRAMENTS

Jan Michael Joncas

Resource Publications, Inc.
San Jose, California

Editorial director: Kenneth Guentert
Editor: Nick Wagner
Managing editor: Elizabeth J. Asborno

Reprint Department
Resource Publications, Inc.
160 E. Virginia St. #290
San Jose, CA 95112-5876

Library of Congress Cataloging in Publications Data
Joncas, Jan Michael, 1951-
  The Catechism of the Catholic Church on liturgy and sacraments / Jan Michael Joncas.
       p.   cm.
  ISBN 0-89390-348-5
  1. Sacraments—Catholic Church. 2. Catholic Church—Liturgy.
3. Catholic Church. Catechismus Ecclesiae Catholicae. 4. Catholic Church—Catechisms. I. Title.
  BX2200.J66 1995
  264'.02—dc20   95-24255

Printed in the United States of America

99 98 97 96 95 | 5 4 3 2 1

Excerpts of this book were originally published in series form in *Modern Liturgy* magazine.

CONTENTS

PREFACE

"Who made you?" "God made me." "Why did God make you?" "God made me to know him and to love him in this life and to be happy with him forever in the next." "What is a sacrament?" "A sacrament is an outward sign instituted by Christ to give grace."

English-speaking Roman Catholics in the United States born in the first half of this century would recognize the dialogues printed above from their encounters with the *Baltimore Catechism*. For a century this document served as the foundational text for the religious education of children as Roman Catholics. With the changes in church life engendered by the Second Vatican Council and with shifts in catechetical theory, memorizing the questions and answers of the *Baltimore Catechism* fell out of practice in most religious education programs during the 1960s.

Though calls for the drafting of a new catechism arose in the closing days of the Second Vatican Council, the new *Catechism of the Catholic Church* [hereafter CCC] directly stems from an Extraordinary Synod convened by Pope John Paul II in 1985. During this synod the presidents of all the bishops' conferences gathered to reflect on the situation of the church twenty years after the close of Vatican II and to chart how the vision and directives of the Council might best be implemented in the years ahead. On 10 July 1986 the Pope entrusted the task of generating a document responsive to the 1985 synod's desires to a commission of twelve prelates with Joseph Cardinal Ratzinger serving as president. Once the commission clarified the literary form of the document as a *catechismus maior* primarily addressed to bishops as the chief overseers of catechesis, the actual text began to appear under the direction of various commission members. (Part Two, treating liturgy and sacraments, was prepared under the guidance of two diocesan bishops, Medina of Chile and Karlic of Argentina.) In 1987 a first draft of the entire CCC was sent to forty consultants, and in 1989 bishops throughout the world received a revised draft for their observations and commentary. The drafting commission approved the definitive French text on 14 February 1992. By the apostolic constitution *Fidei Depositum* (hereafter FD) issued on 11 October 1992 (exactly thirty years after the opening of the Second Vatican Council), Pope John Paul II promulgated the CCC.

In 1994 the English-speaking world received an officially approved translation of the CCC. Unlike the *Baltimore Catechism*, the CCC is not in question-and-answer format but in 2,865 paragraph-length articles, supplemented by indices of citations and subjects. It is not directly addressed to children but rather to Catholic pastors and faithful for the deepening of their faith as well as to interested inquirers who wish to learn what Catholic Christians believe and practice. It is not intended to supplant local catechisms but to encourage and assist in their production.

In the following pages I will examine the liturgical and sacramental teaching of Part Two of the CCC. Both the text (what the document affirms) and its context (how it is structured) will be explored. Since, according to its document of promulgation, the CCC stands as "a sure norm for teaching the faith and a valid and legitimate instrument for ecclesial communion" (FD 4), it is an important source for Roman Catholics to consult as they reflect on the church's faith and action in a changing world.

These reflections began when I was invited by the Archdiocese of St. Paul and Minneapolis to prepare a day-long program for catechists on Part Two of the CCC held in the spring of 1994, based on the French text published in 1992. Sr. Rita Claire Dorner, OP, invited me to refine my ideas for a public lecture at the University of Santa Clara (California) sponsored by the Pastoral Studies Program of the Religious Studies Department in the summer of 1994. Subsequently, *Modern Liturgy*, under the editorial guidance of Nick Wagner, published my considerations of the topic in a series of articles beginning in November 1994. The present work thus distills research and deliberation engaged in over a period of time addressed to diverse audiences. I hope that it will help clergy, catechists, and interested readers of the CCC to appreciate the doctrinal richness of its teaching and to contextualize its affirmations.

I dedicate *The Catechism of the Catholic Church on Liturgy and Sacraments* to my mother, Theresa Joncas. It was from her that I first "learned my catechism." To this day she gives me insight into the meaning of the faith we share.

1. PRELIMINARIES:
STRUCTURE AND SOURCES OF THE CCC

The four-part division of the CCC reflects the division of the *Roman Catechism* (the so-called "Catechism of the Council of Trent"). Part One explores Catholic faith, Part Two corporate worship, Part Three moral reasoning and behavior, and Part Four the life of prayer. While this division has some advantages (historical precedent, ease of reference), it is not the only way in which the CCC could have been organized. Its compilers could have created a "scriptural" catechism, highlighting the Catholic interpretation of the Jewish and Christian scriptures. The authors might have developed a "mystagogical" catechism, drawing the church's doctrine from the church's public prayer. The CCC could have been structured as was the 1983 *Code of Canon Law* around the three *munera* ("tasks," "offices," and "responsibilities") of Christ manifest in the church: prophet (the church teaching), priest (the church sanctifying), and king (the church governing). Its compilers might even have opted for a chronological structure, demonstrating the organic development of the church's teaching. The church's creed, cult, and code are addressed in the CCC. However, the CCC's organization separates corporate prayer (Part Two) and individual prayer (Part Four). This is troublesome insofar as it may reinforce a division between private and communal prayer forms rather than see both as necessary components of the life of faith, mutually influencing and reinforcing each other.

Each major division of the CCC grounds itself in a particular structure: the Creed for Part One, the seven sacraments for Part Two, the Ten Commandments for Part Three, and the Lord's Prayer for Part Four. Again, while there is historical precedent for this structuring, its adequacy remains problematic. Perhaps the greatest criticism of these grounding structures has been raised against the use of the Ten Commandments as the framework to discuss Christian morality: would not the Sermon on the Mount or even the Beatitudes have provided a better framework? Similarly, the choice of the seven sacraments as the grounding structure for exploring the church's public worship makes it difficult to treat topics such as the Liturgy of the Hours, blessings, funerals, monastic profession, or consecration to religious life except by "shoehorning" them in.

The sources of the CCC are many and varied. Sacred scripture hold pride of place. It is not an exaggeration to say that the CCC is saturated with scriptural references, but the use of these references does not always reflect contemporary exegesis. Quotations from ancient Christian writers (the "Fathers") abound; it is especially heartening to see so many citations of Eastern authors. Liturgical prayers are frequently mentioned (again from both Eastern and Western liturgical families) and magisterial teaching (both conciliar and papal, with a strong emphasis on the writings of Pope John Paul II) constantly appears. One drawback is that contemporary theologians are rarely directly quoted.

As noted above, the CCC treats public worship and the seven sacraments of the church in its second part, entitled "The Celebration of the Christian Mystery." After a short introduction sketching the meaning of the term "liturgy" and its relation to Christian life, prayer, and catechesis (1066-1075), Part Two of the CCC comprises two sections: "The Sacramental Economy" (1076-1209) and "The Seven Sacraments of the Church" (1210-1690). The first section, corresponding in some ways to the treatise *"De sacramentis in genere,"* emphasizes an understanding of sacramental life stemming from the liturgy of the Eastern rites and the teaching of Vatican II, while the second section, corresponding to the treatise *"De sacramentis in specie,"* explores positions primarily espoused by scholastic theology and the Council of Trent. Thus the CCC reflects the rich heritage of Catholic thinking on the sacraments at the risk of a certain lack of integration between the two sections.

2.

FROM CREED TO CULT (1066-1075)

Articles 1066-1068 signal a transition from Part One to Part Two of the CCC, from discussion of beliefs to description of worship, from creed to cult:

> In the Symbol of the faith the Church confesses the mystery of the Holy Trinity and of the plan of God's "good pleasure" for all creation....Such is the mystery of Christ, revealed and fulfilled in history according to [a] wisely ordered plan....It is this mystery of Christ that the Church proclaims and celebrates in her liturgy so that the faithful may live from it and bear witness to it in the world[.]

This Trinitarian and Christocentric understanding of the church's worship pervades the CCC's treatment of the liturgy and sacraments. Although one might find the CCC's decision to begin with the church's creed and move to the church's worship somewhat problematic in the light of Prosper of Aquitaine's adage *legem credendi lex statuat supplicandi* ("let the law of praying establish the law of believing"), its emphasis on the intimate connection between faith and worship is quite welcome.

After defining the liturgy etymologically ("service on the part of/in favor of the people"), listing its semantic field in the New Testament, and quoting *Sacrosanctum Concilium* (hereafter SC) 7 as magisterial teaching on the topic, the CCC notes the connections between liturgy and evangelization, engagement in the church's mission, and participation in Christ's prayer. Especially important for religious educators is the declaration in article 1075 that outlines the structure of Part Two:

> Liturgical catechesis aims to initiate people into the mystery of Christ (It is "mystagogy.") by proceeding from the visible to the invisible, from the sign to the thing

3

signified, from the "sacraments" to the "mysteries." Such catechesis is to be presented by local and regional catechisms. This Catechism, which aims to serve the whole Church in all the diversity of her rites and cultures, will present what is fundamental and common to the whole Church in the liturgy as mystery and as celebration (*Section One*), and then the seven sacraments and the sacramentals (*Section Two*).

3.
LITURGY AS MYSTERY
AND CELEBRATION (1076-1209)

3.1. THE SACRAMENTAL ECONOMY (1076-1134)

The CCC wisely founds all sacramental life in the work of the Holy Trinity. God the Father acts as the source and goal of all liturgical worship, a worship that is fundamentally *blessing*:

> 1110 In the liturgy of the Church, God the Father is blessed and adored as the source of all the blessings of creation and of salvation with which he has blessed us in his Son, in order to give us the Spirit of filial adoption.

Grounded in the Jewish *berakah* (a prayer form by which life, time, and space are all referred back to their Source), Christian blessing has a dual dimension. On the one hand, the church united to Christ and under the impetus of the Spirit blesses the Father in adoration, praise, and thanksgiving for his manifold gifts. On the other hand, the church offers the Father its own gifts, asking the Father to send the Holy Spirit upon them, upon the church itself, upon the faithful, and upon the entire world.

According to the CCC the work of Christ in liturgical worship is threefold:

> 1111 Christ's work in the liturgy is sacramental: because his mystery of salvation is made present there by the power of his Holy Spirit; because his Body, which is the Church, is like a sacrament (sign and instrument) in which the Holy Spirit dispenses the mystery of salvation; and because through her liturgical actions the pilgrim Church already participates, as by a foretaste, in the heavenly liturgy.

5

The actions of the earthly Jesus—preaching, teaching, healing, exorcizing, performing miracles, calling people to discipleship—all reveal and embody the reign of God; these actions are brought to perfection in the paschal mystery of his death and resurrection. The risen Christ confides the saving power of his actions to the church, where he is present in a variety of modes: in the sacrifice of the Mass, in the person of the minister, in the eucharistic species, in sacramental actions, in the proclamation and preaching of his word, and in the church gathered, praying, and singing (cf. SC 7). Christ's salvation of the world, accomplished once for all in his sacrificial death on the cross, is made effectively present in the sacramental life.

The CCC also specifies the proper missions of the Holy Spirit in the church's liturgical worship:

> 1112 The mission of the Holy Spirit in the liturgy of the Church is to prepare the assembly to encounter Christ; to recall and manifest Christ to the faith of the assembly; to make the saving work of Christ present and active by his transforming power; and to make the gift of communion bear fruit in the church.

The Spirit prepares the assembly to encounter Christ principally by illuminating their understanding of the Old Testament, disclosing in the reading of these scriptures, in the praying of the psalms, and in the memory of God's saving events—promise of covenant, Passover and Exodus, Kingdom and Temple, Exile and Return—the mystery of Christ in anticipation. The Spirit is the living memory of the church, assisting proclaimers and readers of the New Testament to receive it as powerful witness and not as a "dead letter"; in the Spirit liturgical memorial (*anamnesis*) is not so much simple recollection of past events as encounter with a living presence. The transforming power of the Spirit is invoked (*epiclesis*) upon sacramental signs and symbols, the church and its members, as well as the world in order to extend the saving power of Christ's work. Finally, the Spirit's mission is to bring all into genuine communion as members of Christ's body, an organic union of life and activity.

Thus sacramental life is a genuine sharing, under a complex ordering of signs and symbols, in the very life of the Trinity.

In a paragraph highly reminiscent of the definition of a sacrament in the *Baltimore Catechism*, the CCC states:

> 1131 The sacraments are efficacious signs of grace, instituted by Christ and entrusted to the Church, by which divine life is dispensed to us. The visible rites by which the sacraments are celebrated signify and make present the graces proper to each sacrament. They bear fruit in those who receive them with the required dispositions.

The CCC clarifies the meaning of this rather dense definition of the sacraments in general under five headings: these ritual actions are sacraments 1) of Christ; 2) of the church; 3) of faith; 4) of salvation; and 5) of life eternal.

Sacraments of Christ. Under the heading "sacraments of Christ," the CCC affirms that the sacraments have been instituted by Christ. "Institution" in contemporary theological thought does not mean that Christ intended the specific matter and form for each of the seven sacraments but that the salvific words and actions of Christ—his "mysteries"—are foundational and irreplaceable for the church's sacramental life in the power of the Holy Spirit. As St. Leo the Great asserted in his *Sermon 74*: "That which was visible in our Savior has passed over into his sacraments."

Sacraments of the Church. Instituted by Christ, sacraments have been confided to the church in the dual sense that they are "from the church" and "for the church." They are "from the church" because the church itself is the sacrament of Christ at work in it through the Holy Spirit; they are "for the church" because the sacraments, especially the Eucharist, manifest and communicate to human beings the mystery of communion in divine love, the very life of the Trinity.

Sacraments of Faith. The sacraments presuppose faith. In fact, according to the definition quoted above, faith is one of the "dispositions" required of the recipient in order that the sacrament be "fruitful." Yet celebrating the sacraments also

7

nourishes, strengthens, and expresses faith. It should be noted that the faith of the church is prior to the faith of the individual; the individual is invited to adhere to the church's faith, received from the apostles and proclaimed in sacramental worship. Participating in and reflecting upon sacramental experience should lead the individual Christian to deeper and richer personal faith.

Sacraments of Salvation. Instituted by Christ and confided to the church, these sacraments of faith are *efficacious*, i.e., they confer the grace that they signify. They are effective because in them Christ is at work: in the sacrament of baptism it is Christ who baptizes, in penance it is Christ who reconciles, in holy orders it is Christ who permanently configures members of the faithful for particular ministry. A traditional Catholic understanding of this sacramental efficacy was expressed in the phrase *ex opere operato*, i.e., that the sacraments brought about what they signified not because of the merits of the minister or the recipient but because of Christ, who was at work in them. The church goes so far as to state that for believers the sacraments of the New Law are necessary for salvation because they are the principal means by which the Holy Spirit conforms human beings to Christ. The ultimate result of the sacramental life is that the Holy Spirit "deifies" the faithful by uniting them totally to the Only-Begotten, the Savior.

Sacraments of Life Eternal. Finally, celebrating the sacraments gives a foretaste in the present of the life of the world to come. Sacramental life is the pledge and down payment of the life of the reign of God, a contemporary participation in the end of history. St. Thomas Aquinas highlighted the eschatological dimension of the sacramental life in a formulation that has become classic:

> [A] sacrament is a sign that commemorates what precedes it—Christ's passion; demonstrates what is accomplished in us through Christ's passion—grace; and prefigures what the Passion pledges us to—future glory [*Summa Theologiae* III.60.3.Response].

3.2. THE SACRAMENTAL CELEBRATION
OF THE PASCHAL MYSTERY (1135-1209)

Presuming the foregoing exploration of the "sacramental economy," the CCC then calls attention to "sacramental celebration" under four headings: 1) Who celebrates? 2) How do they celebrate? 3) When do they celebrate? and 4) Where do they celebrate?

Those Who Celebrate Sacramentally. A strong conviction of Roman Catholic Christianity is that the liturgy is celebrated by "the entire Christ—Head and members" [cf. SC 7]. "Thus Christ is the principal agent of sacramental worship. Through the power of the Holy Spirit the church joins Christ in the worship he offers to the Father through all eternity."

In considering the sacramental worship offered by the "members of Christ," the CCC distinguishes between the celebrants of the heavenly liturgy (the angels and saints as well as the transformed created order) and the celebrants of the earthly liturgy (the community of the baptized hierarchically ordered):

> 1187 The liturgy is the work of the whole Christ, head and body. Our high priest celebrates it unceasingly in the heavenly liturgy, with the holy Mother of God, the apostles, all the saints, and the multitude of those who have already entered the kingdom.

> 1188 In a liturgical celebration, the entire assembly is *leitourgos*, each member according to his own function. The baptismal priesthood is that of the whole Body of Christ. But some of the faithful are ordained through the sacrament of Holy Orders to represent Christ as head of the Body.

The Means of Sacramental Celebration. Sacramental celebration takes place by means of signs and symbols. Since human beings unite corporeal and spiritual dimensions of existence, they perceive and express spiritual realities through material elements. Some signs and symbols are taken from nature (e.g., day and night, wind and fire, water and earth, trees and fruit) while others arise from human social life (e.g., washing, massaging with oil, sharing a meal). Some signs and symbols developed in the religious culture of Judaism (e.g., circumcision, consecration of kings and priests, imposition of hands, sacrifices, the Passover), some of which Jesus employed and transformed. Both words and gestures can have sacramental import, the actions signifying what the words express. Music and singing, sacred art and artifacts all furnish important elements in sacramental celebration. As the CCC summarizes:

> 1189 The liturgical celebration involves signs and symbols relating to creation..., human life...and the history of salvation....Integrated into the world of faith and taken up by the power of the Holy Spirit, these cosmic elements, these human rites, and these gestures of remembrance of God become bearers of the saving and sanctifying action of Christ.

The Times of Sacramental Celebration. Just as the events of human living can become carriers of sacramental meaning, so the structuring of time can disclose God's presence to the life of faith. After discussing the notion of liturgical time in general, the CCC discusses the weekly, yearly, and daily dimensions of liturgical worship.

Celebrating the *Lord's Day* once a week is foundational to the Christian structuring of time:

> 1193 Sunday, the "Lord's Day," is the principal day for the celebration of the Eucharist because it is the day of the Resurrection. It is the pre-eminent day of the liturgical assembly, the day of the Christian family, and the day of joy and rest from work. Sunday is "the foundation and kernel of the whole liturgical year" (SC 106).

It should be noted that in the Christian structuring of time, the celebration of the Lord's Day begins with Vespers on Saturday (traditionally associated with sunset), thus connecting the Christian and the Jewish keeping of time. Sunday, however, is *not* a "Christian Sabbath" but the "eighth day," the end-time signaled by the resurrection of Jesus, the first day of a new and endless week no longer grounded in the seven day creation narrative. The claims made for the Lord's Day frequently come into conflict with a late twentieth-century structuring of time that divides "work week" from "weekend."

The *liturgical year* celebrates the mysteries of Christ both in paschal and incarnation cycles as well as in the annual commemoration of saints' feasts:

> 1194 The Church, "in the course of the year,...unfolds the whole mystery of Christ from his Incarnation and Nativity through his Ascension, to Pentecost and the expectation of the blessed hope of the coming of the Lord" (SC 102 § 2).

> 1195 By keeping the memorials of the saints—first of all the holy Mother of God, then the apostles, the martyrs, and other saints—on fixed days of the liturgical year, the Church on earth shows that she is united with the liturgy of heaven. She gives glory to Christ for having accomplished his salvation in his glorified members; their example encourages her on her way to the Father.

The *liturgical day* is marked by prayer at fixed hours, especially the "hinge" hours of Lauds and Vespers, in the Liturgy of the Hours:

> 1196 The faithful who celebrate the Liturgy of the Hours are united to Christ our high priest, by the prayer of the Psalms, meditation on the Word of God, and canticles and blessings, in order to be joined with his unceasing and universal prayer that gives glory to the Father and implores the gift of the Holy Spirit on the whole world.

While many Roman Catholics have little experience of the Liturgy of the Hours, associating it with the breviary obligation of bishops, priests, and deacons and the common choral prayer of monks and nuns, the Second Vatican Council encouraged all the faithful to join in this prayer as the circumstances of their life allowed, since "the divine office is the voice of the Church, that is, of the whole Mystical Body publicly praising God" [SC 99].

The Places of Sacramental Celebration. In addition to human life and time, space itself can become a bearer of sacramental meaning. While the term "church" most properly refers to the gathering of those who share the life of Jesus in baptism, it is also frequently applied to the architectural structure in which those followers gather. The "house of the church" can contain many places and objects by which sacramental worship is enacted: the altar or Lord's Table, the tabernacle, the place of reservation for the blessed oils (chrism, oil of catechumens, oil of the sick), the lectern or ambo for proclaiming God's word, the presidential chair (or the bishop's throne in the cathedral church), the baptismal font and its surrounding baptistry, the confessional or reconciliation room. These places and objects tie the worshiping assembly to the celestial worship celebrated beyond time and space:

> 1197 Christ is the true temple of God, "the place where his glory dwells"; by the grace of God, Christians also become temples of the Holy Spirit, living stones out of which the Church is built.
>
> 1198 In its earthly state the Church needs places where the community can gather together. Our visible churches, holy places, are images of the holy city, the heavenly Jerusalem, toward which we are making our way on pilgrimage.
>
> 1199 It is in these churches that the Church celebrates public worship to the glory of the Holy Trinity, hears the word of God and sings his praise, lifts up her prayer, and offers the sacrifice of Christ sacramentally present in the midst of the assembly. These churches are also places of recollection and personal prayer.

4.

THE SEVEN SACRAMENTS
AND SACRAMENTALS (1210-1666)

After discussing sacramental life in general, the CCC turns to a treatment of individual sacraments. Its treatment of the sacraments, though remarkably broad in scope, raises certain problems. Consider the following articles:

> 1210 Christ instituted the sacraments of the new law. There are seven: Baptism, Confirmation (or Chrismation), the Eucharist, Penance, the Anointing of the Sick, Holy Orders and Matrimony. The seven sacraments touch all the stages and all the important moments of Christian life: they give birth and increase, healing and mission to the Christian's life of faith. There is thus a certain resemblance between the stages of natural life and the stages of the spiritual life.

> 1211 Following this analogy,...the three sacraments of Christian initiation [will be treated first, followed by]...the sacraments of healing [, and finally]...the sacraments at the service of communion and the mission of the faithful. This order, while not the only one possible, does allow one to see that the sacraments form an organic whole in which each particular sacrament has its own vital place. In this organic whole, the Eucharist occupies a unique place as the "Sacrament of sacraments": "all the other sacraments are ordered to it as to their end."

First of all, the CCC, while confirming traditional Catholic teaching that the sacraments were "instituted" by Christ, does not address the questions surrounding this "institution": how and when it took place, what warrants exist for the church's position, and how they are to be interpreted. Second, the CCC affirms the seven-fold numbering of the sacraments without attending to the variety of enumerations present earlier in the church's history (e.g., Peter Damian, who listed twelve sacraments), the numbering given by other ecclesial bodies (e.g., the two or three "dominical" sacraments of Lutheranism), or contemporary speculation (e.g., the diaconate as an "eighth" sacrament,[1] the humanity of Christ as "sacrament-of-God," the church as "sacrament-of-Christ"). Thirdly, the choice to organize the sacramental system by an analogy to natural life, while certainly reflecting Thomas Aquinas' treatment in the *Summa Theologiae*, may prejudice the treatment of individual sacraments (e.g., Confirmation as a "sacrament of Christian maturity") as well as promote an unduly individualistic understanding of the effects of the sacraments. Fourth, relegating the treatment of the Eucharist to the chapter on the sacraments of initiation distorts its position in the sacramental economy; this organization is especially surprising since the CCC itself affirms that:

> 1324 The Eucharist is "the source and summit of the Christian life" [*Lumen gentium* 11]. "The other sacraments, and indeed all ecclesiastical ministries and works of the apostolate, are bound up with the Eucharist and

---

[1] "The division of order into the three degrees of episcopacy, presbyterate, and diaconate is not well served by the appeal to the category of priesthood or by the ahistorical reading of church development. Though the document has distinguished order from baptism in terms of the different participations in the priesthood of Christ, it finds ministerial priesthood verified only in the episcopacy and the presbyterate, not the diaconate....The deacon is said to receive a distinct sacramental character that configures him to Christ the servant of all....Logically this would make the diaconate either a distinct sacrament or not a sacrament at all if the only distinction is between types of priesthood. What the document ends up with are: the baptismal priesthood, the ministerial priesthood, and the diaconate, which has a unique (sacramental) character of service. This logically means an economy of eight, not seven, sacraments" (David N. Power, "The Sacraments in the Catechism," in *The Universal Catechism Reader: Reflections and Responses*, ed. Thomas J. Reese [San Francisco: HarperSanFrancisco, 1990], 122.)

are oriented toward it. For in the blessed Eucharist is contained the whole spiritual good of the Church, namely, Christ himself, our Pasch" [*Presbyterorum ordinis* 5].

Fifth, the ecclesiological implications and pneumatological underpinnings of the sacramental economy tend to be underplayed. In addition to presenting the sacraments as actions of the body of Christ united in the Spirit manifesting and celebrating its reality as church in Section One, the CCC continues to present sacramental actions in terms of (individual) minister(s) and (individual) recipient(s) throughout Section Two.

Having raised these issues, we should also note two structural decisions made by the CCC's authors for Section Two. First, although the treatment of the seven sacraments follows the ordering of the "natural life" analogy mentioned above, they are grouped into three categories: sacraments of initiation, sacraments of healing, and sacraments of service to communion; this format nuances the simple presentation of the sacraments in relation to individual human development. Second, each sacrament is treated under categories familiar to scholastic theology; after exploring the terms used to refer to the sacrament and its scriptural foundations, the CCC considers the fundamental constituents ("matter" and "form"), recipients, ministers, and effects of each sacrament. It is heartening to note that the CCC provides a "mystagogy" for each of the sacraments, attempting to draw its sacramental theology from the actual celebration of the rites.

5.

THE SACRAMENTS OF INITIATION
(1212-1419)

Article 1212 provides the rationale for considering baptism, confirmation, and Eucharist as a unit:

> 1212 The sacraments of Christian initiation—Baptism, Confirmation, and the Eucharist—lay the *foundations* of every Christian life. "The sharing in the divine nature given to men through the grace of Christ bears a certain likeness to the origin, development, and nourishing of natural life. The faithful are born anew by Baptism, strengthened by the sacrament of Confirmation, and receive in the Eucharist the food of eternal life. By means of these sacraments of Christian initiation, they thus receive in increasing measure the treasures of the divine life and advance toward the perfection of charity" [Paul VI: Apostolic Constitution, *Divinae consortium naturae*].

It should be noted that, like the 1983 *Code of Canon Law* and the *praenotanda* to each of the post-Vatican II reformed rites of initiation, the CCC presents the order of the initiation sacraments as baptism/confirmation/Eucharist. While acknowledging that baptism forms the indispensable foundation for Christian initiation, the document affirms that confirmation and Eucharist form its necessary completion:

> 1306 ...Since Baptism, Confirmation, and Eucharist form a unity, it follows that "the faithful are obliged to receive this sacrament at the appropriate time," for without Confirmation and Eucharist, Baptism is certainly valid and efficacious, but Christian initiation remains incomplete.

> 1322 The holy Eucharist completes Christian initiation. Those who have been raised to the dignity of the royal

priesthood by Baptism and configured more deeply to Christ by Confirmation participate with the whole community in the Lord's own sacrifice by means of the Eucharist.

5.1. BAPTISM (1213-1284)

The CCC's treatment of baptism begins with a rich description and definition ultimately derived from the teaching of the Council of Florence:

> 1213 Holy Baptism is the basis of the whole Christian life, the gateway to life in the Spirit (*vitae spiritualis ianua*), and the door which gives access to the other sacraments. Through Baptism we are freed from sin and reborn as sons of God; we become members of Christ, are incorporated into the Church and made sharers in her mission: "Baptism is the sacrament of regeneration through water in the word" [Augustine: *De catechizandis rudibus* 2.2.5].

It then notes the various terms used to refer to this sacrament in Christian history, each revealing a different nuance of its meaning: "plunging," "immersion," "bath of regeneration and rebirth," "enlightenment," "anointing," "garment," "seal." Presenting the scriptural foundations for the sacrament, the CCC explains the "prefigurings" of baptism in the Old Testament by commenting on the references in the blessing of the baptismal water at the Easter Vigil, explores New Testament teaching on Jesus' baptism by John (though it omits mention of the controverted passage in which Jesus himself was said to have baptized during his public ministry), explains the risen Christ's command to baptize all nations (Mt 28:19-20) as the foundation for the sacramental life typified in the blood and water flowing from the Crucified One's side (Jn 19:24), and notes how this command was obeyed by the early church, both in the initiations recorded in the Acts of the Apostles and in the theological reflection on baptism produced by Paul and the author of 1 Peter.

The CCC's treatment of how the sacrament is celebrated is notable not only for its recognition of differing processes of initiation for adults and infants but its articulation of constituent aspects of Christian initiation configured in various ways in Eastern and Western liturgical traditions:

> 1229 From the time of the apostles, becoming a Christian has been accomplished by a journey and initiation in several stages. This journey can be covered rapidly or slowly, but certain essential elements will always have to be present: proclamation of the Word, acceptance of the Gospel entailing conversion, profession of faith, Baptism itself, the outpouring of the Holy Spirit, and admission to Eucharistic communion.

> 1230 This initiation has varied greatly through the centuries according to circumstances. In the first centuries of the Church, Christian initiation saw considerable development. A long period of *catechumenate* included a series of preparatory rites, which were liturgical landmarks along the path of catechumenal preparation and culminated in the celebration of the sacraments of Christian initiation.

> 1231 Where infant Baptism has become the form in which this sacrament is usually celebrated, it has become a single act encapsulating the preparatory stages of Christian initiation in a very abridged way. By its very nature infant Baptism requires a *post-baptismal catechumenate*. Not only is there a need for instruction after Baptism, but also for the necessary flowering of baptismal grace in personal growth....

> 1233 Today in all the rites, Latin and Eastern, the Christian initiation of adults begins with their entry into the catechumenate and reaches its culmination in a single celebration of the three sacraments of initiation: Baptism, Confirmation, and the Eucharist. In the Eastern rites the Christian initiation of infants also begins with Baptism followed immediately by Confirmation and the Eucharist,

while in the Roman rite it is followed by years of catechesis before being completed later by Confirmation and the Eucharist, the summit of their Christian initiation.

Though one could question the propriety of the term "post-baptismal catechumenate," the CCC's strong emphasis on the necessity of nurturing Christian belief and practice in those baptized at infancy should make it clear that infant baptism is not magical or superstitious. I suspect that some Western rite communities, however, will begin to question if imitating the Eastern practice of celebrating the rites of initiation as a unity for infants as well as for adults should not be adopted.

Articles 1234 through 1245 provide a model "mystagogy" of baptism, sketching the significance of the sign of the cross, the Liturgy of the Word, pre-baptismal exorcism(s), anointing with the oil of catechumens, profession of the Creed, the triple immersion (indicated as the preferred form) or pouring of water with accompanying sacramental formula (given in both Western and Eastern forms), anointing with chrism, clothing in a white garment, presentation of a baptismal candle, first communion (or praying of the Lord's Prayer), and solemn blessing. Though the explanations provided in the CCC are cursory, they should help catechists to ground their sacramental reflections in the actual rites celebrated.

Declaring that "[e]very person not yet baptized and only such a person is able to be baptized" (1246), the CCC distinguishes the baptism of adults from that of infants, clarifying in the process the status of catechumens as members of the "household of Christ" though not yet initiated Christians, the roles played by Christian parents in bringing their infants for baptism, and the responsibilities of godparents.

The CCC affirms traditional Roman Catholic teaching that the ordinary ministers of baptism are bishops and presbyters (as well as deacons in the Western churches), but in case of necessity baptized laity or even an unbaptized person can validly baptize if he/she uses water and the Trinitarian formula and intends to do what the church intends in baptizing.

In its discussion of the necessity of baptism, the CCC makes two statements with important pastoral consequences. First, while strongly affirming the intrinsic connection between baptism and salvation, the document recognizes that there are those who are saved outside the (Catholic) sacramental system since God's mercy will not be bound:

> 1257 The Lord himself affirms that Baptism is necessary for salvation [cf. Jn 3:5]. He also commands his disciples to proclaim the Gospel to all nations and to baptize them [cf. Mt 28:19-20]. Baptism is necessary for salvation for those to whom the Gospel has been proclaimed and who have had the possibility of asking for this sacrament [cf. Mk 16:16]. The Church does not know of any means other than Baptism that assures entry into eternal beatitude; this is why she takes care not to neglect the mission she has received from the Lord to see that all those who can be baptized are "reborn of water and the Spirit." *God has bound salvation to the sacrament of Baptism, but he himself is not bound by his sacraments.*

Second, after discussing the categories of "baptism of blood" and "baptism of desire," the CCC treats the situation of infants dying without receiving water baptism:

> 1261 As regards *children who have died without Baptism,* the Church can only entrust them to the mercy of God, as she does in her funeral rites for them. Indeed, the great mercy of God who desires that all men should be saved [cf. 1 Tm 2:4], and Jesus' tenderness toward children which caused him to say: "Let the children come to me, do not hinder them" [Mk 10:14], allow us to hope that there is a way of salvation for children who have died without Baptism. All the more urgent is the Church's call not to prevent little children coming to Christ through the gift of holy Baptism.

It is interesting that no mention is made of "limbo" in this context.

The CCC lists the effects of baptism under five major headings: remission of sins, new birth in the Holy Spirit (rendering the person capable of activating the theological and the moral virtues as well as the gifts of the Holy Spirit), incorporation into the church (given a share in the common priesthood of the faithful), founding the unity of Christians, and sealing with an indelible spiritual mark ("baptismal character"), indicating that repetition of validly received baptism is impossible.

5.2. CONFIRMATION (1285-1321)

The CCC begins its treatment of the sacrament of confirmation with a description and definition of the sacrament ultimately derived from *Lumen gentium* 11:

> 1285 Baptism, the Eucharist, and the sacrament of Confirmation together constitute the "sacraments of Christian initiation," whose unity must be safeguarded. It must be explained to the faithful that the reception of the sacrament of Confirmation is necessary for the completion of baptismal grace. For "by the sacrament of Confirmation, [the baptized] are more perfectly bound to the Church and are enriched with a special strength of the Holy Spirit. Hence they are, as true witnesses of Christ, more strictly obliged to spread and defend the faith by word and deed."

The document then declares that what the Old Testament prophets predicted about the Spirit of the Lord resting upon the promised Messiah in view of his saving mission was fulfilled by the descent of the Holy Spirit upon Jesus during his baptism by John: Jesus is revealed as the Anointed One (the "Christ") of God. As risen Lord, Jesus actualizes the outpouring of this Spirit on Easter (Jn 20:22) and on the day of Pentecost (according to Acts 2:1-4). Other New Testament passages, especially taken from the Acts of the Apostles and the Letter to the Hebrews, disclose how the Spirit was further communicated in the primitive church. Both the laying on of hands and anointing with perfumed oil are symbolically connected with the gift of the Spirit. The CCC is to be commended for the restraint with which it treats these scriptural citations; none are declared "prooftexts" for the institution of the sacrament by Christ.

Both Eastern and Western approaches to this sacrament are highlighted:

> 1289 ...[T]he Eastern Churches call this sacrament *Chrismation*, anointing with chrism, or *myron* which means "chrism." In the West, *Confirmation* suggests both the ratification of Baptism, thus completing Christian initiation, and the strengthening of baptismal grace—both fruits of the Holy Spirit.

> 1290 In the first centuries Confirmation generally comprised one single celebration with Baptism, forming with it a "double sacrament," according to the expression of St. Cyprian. Among other reasons, the multiplication of infant baptisms all through the year, the increase of rural parishes, and the growth of dioceses often prevented the bishop from being present at all baptismal celebrations. In the West the desire to reserve the completion of Baptism to the bishop caused the temporal separation of the two sacraments. The East has kept them united, so that Confirmation is conferred by the priest who baptizes. But he can do so only with the "myron" consecrated by a bishop.

> 1292 The practice of the Eastern Churches gives greater emphasis to the unity of Christian initiation. That of the Latin Church more clearly expresses the communion of the new Christian with the bishop as guarantor and servant of the unity, catholicity and apostolicity of his Church, and hence the connection with the apostolic origins of Christ's Church.

The references to confirmation as the "completion" of baptism are problematic since reception of the Eucharist is elsewhere presented as the climax and completion of the sacraments of Christian initiation.

The CCC offers contrasting approaches to the meaning of the sacrament of confirmation. It quotes an Eastern consecration of the myron prayer text and describes the gestures and formulas proper to this rite as well as the Western invocation of the Holy Spirit prayer text with its accompanying gestures and formulas (1297, 1299, 1300). Clearly the "essential rite" is not limited to a single liturgical tradition. The meaning of the sacrament is likewise not confined to a single liturgical tradition. Most of the effects of the sacrament are presented as intensifications of capacities given in baptism: enfolding us more strongly in the divine adoption that allows us to address God as "Abba," uniting us more strongly with Christ, increasing in us the gifts of the Holy Spirit, making our bond with the church more perfect, and giving us a special power to witness to faith in Christ; in addition, like baptism, confirmation imprints an indelible spritual mark ("character") signifying that it can be validly received only once (1303-1305).

According to article 1306, "every baptized person not yet confirmed can and should receive the sacrament of Confirmation," though article 1307 recognizes that the Latin tradition has delayed reception of the sacrament to the "age of discretion." Those who argue for a theological understanding of this sacrament as an adolescent rite of passage or an entrance into Christian adulthood will not find encouragement in the CCC:

> 1308 Although Confirmation is sometimes called the "sacrament of Christian maturity," we must not confuse adult faith with the adult age of natural growth, nor forget that baptismal grace is a grace of free, unmerited election and does not need any "ratification" to become effective....

The differing Eastern and Western approaches to this sacrament also affect the customary minister of the sacrament:

> 1312 The *original minister* of Confirmation is the bishop.
> In the East, ordinarily the priest who baptizes also

immediately confers Confirmation in one and the same celebration. But he does so with sacred chrism consecrated by the patriarch or the bishop, thus expressing the apostolic unity of the Church whose bonds are strengthened by the sacrament of Confirmation. In the Latin Church, the same discipline applies to the Baptism of adults or to the reception into full communion with the Church of a person baptized in another Christian community that does not have valid Confirmation.

1313 In the Latin Rite, the ordinary minister of Confirmation is the bishop. Although the bishop may for grave reasons concede to priests the faculty of administering Confirmation, it is appropriate from the very meaning of the sacrament that he should confer it himself, mindful that the celebration of Confirmation has been temporally separated from Baptism for this reason. Bishops are the successors of the apostles. They have received the fullness of the sacrament of Holy Orders. The administration of this sacrament by them demonstrates clearly that its effect is to unite those who receive it more closely to the Church, to her apostolic origins, and to her mission of bearing witness to Christ.

5.3. EUCHARIST (1322-1419)

Although the CCC attempts to describe and define the Eucharist in articles 1322-1327, the "inexhaustible richness" of the sacrament is more powerfully evoked in the myriad of terms developed in Christian tradition that the document lists: thanksgiving ("eucharist"), Lord's Supper, wedding feast of the Lamb, breaking of bread, eucharistic assembly ("synaxis"), memorial of the Lord's passion and resurrection, holy sacrifice of the Mass, sacrifice of praise, spiritual sacrifice, pure and holy sacrifice, holy and divine liturgy, holy mysteries, most holy sacrament, communion, the holy things (*ta hagia*), bread of angels, bread of heaven, medicine of immortality, viaticum, and the Mass (1328-1332). This profusion of terminology should keep pastors and catechists from attempting to reduce the multivalent symbolism of the Eucharist to a single dimension.

When discussing the scriptural foundations for the Eucharist, the CCC lists "prefigurings" in the bread and wine offered by Melchizedech, the unleavened bread eaten on the eve of the Exodus from Egypt, the manna in the desert wandering after the Exodus, and the "cup of blessing" that concluded the Passover Seder (1333-1334). Although the document strongly grounds the institution of the sacrament of the Eucharist in the Last Supper shared on the night before Jesus was executed, it also notes parallels to the eucharistic meal in the miracle of the multiplication of the loaves (1335, 1337-1339). The intimate connections among the eschatological Kingdom-feast, Christian Eucharist, the Last Supper, and the Jewish Passover are emphasized:

> 1340 By celebrating the Last Supper with his apostles in the course of the Passover meal, Jesus gave the Jewish Passover its definitive meaning. Jesus' passing over to his father by his death and Resurrection, the new Passover, is anticipated in the Supper and celebrated in the Eucharist, which fulfills the Jewish Passover and anticipates the final Passover of the Church in the glory of the kingdom.

The Jewish (*le-zikkaron*) and Christian (*anamnesis*) notions of liturgical memorial are clarified by the CCC. They are clearly greater than a bare mental recalling of past events; rather, the present power of the originating events transforms worshipers in the light of the final consummation and fulfillment these events promise and effect:

> 1341 The command of Jesus to repeat his actions and words "until he comes" does not only ask us to remember Jesus and what he did. It is directed at the liturgical celebration, by the apostles and their successors, of the *memorial* of Christ, of his life, of his death, of his Resurrection, and of his intercession in the presence of the Father.

1363 In the sense of Sacred Scripture the *memorial* is not merely the recollection of past events but the proclamation of the mighty works wrought by God for men. In the liturgical celebration of these events, they become in a certain way present and real.

Thus the difficult notion that *anamnesis* involves "remembering the future" (since the death-resurrection of Christ is not only a past event and a present power but God's future final eschatological word to humankind) enters into this catechetical project.

Perhaps the strongest contribution the CCC makes in its presentation of the sacrament of the Eucharist is its mystagogy on the eucharistic rite. After quoting chapters 65 and 67 of the *First Apology* of Justin Martyr (c. 155 of the Common Era [CE]) to show how the fundamental structure of Christian Eucharist has remained the same from the second century to the present, the document treats the "movement of the celebration": the gathering of the assembly, the Liturgy of the Word, the presentation of the gifts, the anaphora, and communion. Of special interest to catechists is weight placed on explaining the components of the eucharistic prayer:

1352 The *anaphora*: with the Eucharistic Prayer—the prayer of thanksgiving and consecration—we come to the heart and summit of the celebration:

In the *preface*, the Church gives thanks to the Father, through Christ, in the Holy Spirit, for all his works: creation, redemption, and sanctification. The whole community thus joins in the unending praise that the Church in heaven, the angels and all the saints, sing to the thrice-holy God.

1353 In the *epiclesis*, the Church asks the Father to send his Holy Spirit (or the power of his blessing [cf. Roman Canon]) on the bread and wine, so that by his power they may become the body and blood of Jesus Christ and so that those who take part in the Eucharist might be one body and one spirit (some liturgical traditions put the epiclesis after the anamnesis).

In the *institution narrative*, the power of the words and the action of Christ, and the power of the Holy Spirit, make sacramentally present under the species of bread and wine Christ's body and blood, his sacrifice offered on the cross once for all.

1354 In the *anamnesis* that follows, the Church calls to mind the Passion, resurrection and glorious return of Christ Jesus; she presents to the Father the offering of his Son which reconciles us with him.

In the *intercessions*, the Church indicates that the Eucharist is celebrated in communion with the whole Church in heaven and on earth, the living and the dead, and in communion with the pastors of the Church, the Pope, the diocesan bishop, his presbyterium and his deacons, and all the bishops of the whole world together with their Churches.

Though this material will not be new for those familiar with the *General Instruction of the Roman Missal* or the documents issued from the Vatican when promulgating the three universal Roman rite eucharistic prayers, the three eucharistic prayers for use at Masses with children, or the two eucharistic prayers for use in Masses of Reconciliation, its presence in the CCC is quite heartening.

Having explored the ritual celebration of the Eucharist, the CCC now turns to its theological elaboration. Three fundamental notions guide this theological elaboration: the Eucharist as sacramental *sacrifice*, as paschal *banquet*, and as *pledge of future glory*. Some commentators have objected to this ordering, thinking that the sacrificial elements are given undue prominence, but I believe the authors were simply trying to work out the Trinitarian implications of eucharistic worship before turning to an understanding of Eucharist as meal and foretaste.

The Eucharist as sacramental sacrifice is explored under three key notions (thanksgiving, memorial, and presence) yoked to a Trinitarian perspective:

> 1357 We carry out this command of the Lord ["Do this in memory of me" (1 Cor 11:24-25)] by celebrating the *memorial of his sacrifice*. In so doing, *we offer to the Father* what he has himself given us: the gifts of his creation, bread and wine which, by the power of the Holy Spirit and by the words of Christ, have become the body and blood of Christ. Christ is thus really and mysteriously made *present*.

> 1358 We must therefore consider the Eucharist as:

> – thanksgiving and praise to the *Father*;
> – the sacrificial memorial of *Christ* and his Body;
> – the presence of Christ by the power of his word and of his *Spirit*.

In the Eucharist the church blesses the Father for the blessings he bestows and offers the Father praise through Christ and with Christ in order to be accepted in Christ (1359-1361). Because it is the *anamnesis* of Christ's Passover, the Eucharist is also a sacrifice, re-presenting the sacrifice of the cross and conjoining the sacrifices of the members of the church to the uniquely efficacious sacrifice of Christ (1362-1372). Through the power of the Holy Spirit Christ is made present to the church in multiple modes: in his Word, in the prayer of two or three gathered in his name, in the poor and the sick, in prisoners, in the sacraments he administers, in the person of his ministers, and in the sacrifice of the Mass (1373). The CCC highlights the unique form of Christ's presence in the eucharistic species, affirms the propriety of describing the conversion of these elements as *transubstantiation*, and notes the custom of reserving the consecrated species for communion of the sick, viaticum, and as a focus of devotional prayer (1374-1379).

Considering the Eucharist as paschal banquet allows the CCC to sketch the various forms of sacramental communion in Eastern and Western traditions. It then enumerates the fruits of sacramental communion: a deepened union with Christ, a separation from sin (helping us to avoid mortal sin and actually effacing venial sins), a yoking of the baptized into the mystical body of Christ, an impetus to action on behalf of the poor, and a genuine foundation for union among all Christians (1382-1398).

Finally the CCC affirms the eschatological character of every eucharistic celebration:

> 1405 There is no surer pledge or clearer sign of this great hope in the new heavens and new earth "in which righteousness dwells" [2 Pet 3:13], than the Eucharist. Every time this mystery is celebrated, "the work of our redemption is carried on" and we "break the one bread that provides the medicine of immortality, the antidote for death, and the food that makes us live for ever in Jesus Christ" [*Lumen gentium* 3].

6.

THE SACRAMENTS OF HEALING
(1420-1532)

The CCC categorizes two of the seven sacraments it treats under the heading "sacraments of healing." The need for such sacraments arises from human fragility; the purpose of these sacraments is to manifest the merciful power of Christ over both sin and sickness:

> 1420 Through the sacraments of Christian initiation, man receives the new life of Christ. Now we carry this life "in "earthen vessels" [2 Cor 4:7], and it remains "hidden with Christ in God" [Col 3:3]. We are still in our "earthly tent" (2 Cor 5:1), subject to suffering, illness, and death. This new life as a child of God can be weakened and even lost by sin.

> 1421 The Lord Jesus Christ, physician of our souls and bodies, who forgave the sins of the paralytic and restored him to bodily health [cf. Mk 2:1-12], has willed that his Church continue, in the power of the Holy Spirit, his work of healing and salvation, even among her own members. This is the purpose of the two sacraments of healing: the sacrament of Penance and the sacrament of Anointing of the Sick.

A later article in this section (1525) will yoke viaticum with these two sacraments as a parallel with the three sacraments of Christian initiation.

6.1. PENANCE/RECONCILIATION (1422-1498)

Following the pattern set for the treatment of individual sacraments in the CCC, the document defines and describes the sacrament, surveys the terminology associated with it,

Pages
24 - 29

seeks its foundation and development in the scriptures and history of the church, presents its essential constituents, recipients, ministers, and effects, and sketches its liturgical celebration. Somewhat surprisingly, a treatment of indulgences is also inserted into the CCC's treatment of penance.

Lumen gentium 11 provides the definition and description of the sacrament of penance founding the CCC's treatment:

> 1422 "Those who approach the sacrament of Penance obtain pardon from God's mercy for the offense committed against him, and are, at the same time, reconciled with the Church which they have wounded by their sins and which by charity, by example, and by prayer labors for their conversion."

But the various terms listed for the sacrament show how complex a reality it is: it is a sacrament "of conversion," "penance," "confession," "pardon," and "reconciliation" (1423-1424). Most interestingly, the CCC notes that "confession" denotes not only the penitent's listing of sins but "the recognition and praise of the holiness of God and of his mercy toward sinful human beings," a wonderful recapturing of the semantic field of *exomologesis* ("confession" not only of sins but of God's merciful forgiveness).

A lengthy section of the CCC's presentation on this sacrament (1425-1439) responds to the question: "Why a sacrament of reconciliation after baptism?" Properly noting that *conversion* to Christ is the keynote of the Christian life, the document clarifies that such conversion is properly signaled and shaped by the sacraments of Christian initiation. But because of *concupiscence*, here defined as the inclination to sin arising from the fragility and weakness of human nature, the baptized may fall away from the life of grace, partially or totally. Thus a *(second) conversion* of the baptized is a necessary component of Christian life:

> 1428 Christ's call to conversion continues to resound in the lives of Christians. This *second conversion* is an

31

uninterrupted task for the whole Church who, "clasping sinners to her bosom, [is] at once holy and always in need of purification, [and] follows constantly the path of penance and renewal" [*Lumen gentium* 8]. This endeavor of conversion is not just a human work. It is the movement of a "contrite heart" [Ps 51:17], drawn and moved by grace to respond to the merciful love of God who loved us first.

The CCC is quite straightforward in asserting that this second conversion is manifest in various ways in addition to the sacrament of penance. What is important above all is "interior repentance," without which acts of penance are sterile and lifeless:

> 1431 Interior repentance is a radical reorientation of our whole life, a return, a conversion to God with all our heart, an end of sin, a turning away from evil, with repugnance toward the evil actions we have committed. At the same time it entails the desire and resolution to change one's life, with hope in God's mercy and trust in the help of his grace. This conversion of heart is accompanied by a salutary pain and sadness which the Fathers called *animi cruciatus* (affliction of spirit) and *compunctio cordis* (repentance of heart).

Impelled by interior penance, however, sinners manifest conversion in multiple ways: the traditional disciplines of prayer, fasting, and almsgiving; martyrdom; efforts to reconcile oneself with one's neighbor; tears; anxiety for the salvation of the neighbor; practice of charity; actions of reconciliation; care for the poor; the exercise and defense of justice and of the right; avowal of faults to one's brothers and sisters; fraternal correction; revision of life; examination of conscience; spiritual direction; acceptance of suffering; endurance of persecution for the cause of justice. Participation in the Eucharist, reading sacred scripture, the prayer of the Liturgy of the Hours and of the Lord's Prayer, all sincere acts of worship or of piety, days of penance during the course of the liturgical year (the season of Lent, each Friday in memory of the death of the Lord), spiritual exercises, penitential liturgies, and pilgrimages can also be expressions of interior penance (1434-1439).

It is in the context of specifying the primacy of conversion and its multiple expressions in Christian life that the CCC discusses the sacrament of penance:

> 1440 Sin is before all else an offense against God, a rupture of communion with him. At the same time it damages communion with the Church. For this reason conversion entails both God's forgiveness and reconciliation with the Church, which are expressed and accomplished liturgically by the sacrament of Penance and Reconciliation.

Two truths must be held simultaneously in any catechetical exploration of the sacrament of penance: God *alone* pardons sin (the church and the minister mediate rather than produce this pardon in sacramental activity), and reconciliation with God and reconciliation with the church are intimately tied.

The CCC provides a whirlwind tour of the changes in forms of celebration of this sacrament in article 1447, claiming in all the diversity that the following fundamental structure can be discerned:

> 1448 ...It comprises two equally essential elements: on the one hand, the acts of the man who undergoes conversion through the action of the Holy Spirit: namely, contrition, confession and satisfaction; on the other, God's action through the intervention of the Church. The Church, who through the bishop and his priests forgives sins in the name of Jesus Christ and determines the manner of satisfaction, also prays for the sinner and does penance with him. Thus the sinner is healed and re-established in ecclesial communion.

Later articles then specify the fundamental importance for the penitent of contrition (categorized as "perfect" or "imperfect" [1451-1454]), of confession of mortal sins as strictly necessary (though confession of venial sins is recommended [1455-

1458]), and of satisfaction (manifest in prayer, offering, works of mercy, service to the neighbor, voluntary privations, sacrifices, and above all our patient bearing of one's cross in imitation of the Lord [1459-1460]).

Three pastoral concerns arise in this section. First, in discussing the penitent's preparation for the sacrament of penance, the CCC suggests:

> 1454 The reception of this sacrament ought to be prepared for by an *examination of conscience* made in the light of the Word of God. The passages best suited to this can be found in the moral catechesis of the Gospels and the apostolic Letters, such as the Sermon on the Mount and the apostolic teachings.

For many, the examination of conscience has been structured around the Ten Commandments, and the CCC wisely recognizes that the Christian moral life cannot be adequately assessed solely in reference to the Decalogue.

Second, quoting the Council of Trent, the CCC requires integral confession of mortal sins to the confessor in number and kind:

> 1456 Confession to a priest is an essential part of the sacrament of Penance: "All mortal sins of which penitents after a diligent self-examination are conscious must be recounted by them in confession, even if they are most secret and have been committed against the last two precepts of the Decalogue [cf. Ex 20:17; Mt 5:28]; for these sins sometimes wound the soul more grievously and are more dangerous than those which are committed openly."

Without challenging this teaching, I would simply note that one of the three forms of this sacrament appearing in the post-Vatican II reformed liturgical books is a rite for communal reconciliation *without individual confession of sins* followed by general absolution (Form III). Admittedly, disciplinary regulations restrict this rite to quasi-emergency settings, but, strictly speaking, not every celebration of penance calls for a disclosure of mortal sins in number and kind to a confessor during the rite. (Form III does exhort penitents receiving general absolution without individual confession to go to individual confession "as soon as they have the opportunity before any further reception of general absolution".) A deeper question arises when one considers the practice of the Eastern church in which the confessor questions the penitent about life-practices in order to mutually discover what is genuinely sinful: part of the horror of sin is that penitents' judgments may be so clouded by sin that they are not even able to identify what is genuinely mortally sinful in their lives, let alone enumerate and categorize these sins.

Third, quoting canon 914 of the 1983 *Code of Canon Law*, article 1457 declares, "Children must go to the sacrament of Penance before receiving Holy Communion for the first time." One presumes that the CCC is here talking only about children baptized in infancy who have yet to receive the sacraments of confirmation and Eucharist, not children of catechetical age who will receive baptism, confirmation, and Eucharist in a single ceremony. My understanding is that the church properly demands *catechesis* on the sacrament of penance for such children before their first communion but that it does not require the children to actually receive the sacrament. This is for the simple reason that the sacrament is only strictly required for those conscious of committing mortal sin, and the church does not and cannot presume that children about to receive first communion have committed mortal sins. On the other hand, if the child chooses to receive the sacrament prior to first communion, the child cannot be prevented from doing so. A parallel I make is to the sacrament of the anointing of the sick: prior to first communion, the child should learn through catechesis that the church offers such a sacrament, but one would not demand that the child receive anointing before first communion unless there was an actual need for it in the child's life.

Noting that the ministry of this sacrament has been confided to bishops and presbyters, the CCC sketches the attitudes and virtues necessary in a good confessor:

1465 When he celebrates the sacrament of Penance, the priest is fulfilling the ministry of the Good Shepherd who seeks the lost sheep, of the Good Samaritan who binds up wounds, of the Father who awaits the prodigal son and welcomes him on his return, and of the just and impartial judge whose judgment is both just and merciful. The priest is the sign and the instrument of God's merciful love for the sinner.

1466 The confessor is not the master of God's forgiveness, but its servant. The minister of this sacrament should unite himself to the intention and charity of Christ. He should have a proven knowledge of Christian behavior, experience of human affairs, respect and sensitivity toward the one who has fallen; he must love the truth, be faithful to the Magisterium of the Church, and lead the penitent with patience toward healing and full maturity. He must pray and do penance for his penitent, entrusting him to the Lord's mercy.

Such sage pastoral advice contextualizes the CCC's teaching on excommunication and the absolute secrecy surrounding the "seal of confession" treated in this same section.

The clearest statement of the effects of the sacrament appears in the summary sentences that conclude each subsection of the CCC:

1496 The spiritual effects of the sacrament of Penance are:

- reconciliation with God by which the penitent recovers grace;
- reconciliation with the Church;
- remission of the eternal punishment incurred by mortal sins;
- remission, at least in part, of temporal punishments resulting from sin;
- peace and serenity of conscience, and spiritual consolation;
- an increase of spiritual strength for the Christian battle.

The CCC devotes nine articles to the topic of indulgences (1471-1479). Defined as "total or partial remission of the temporal punishment due to sin(s)," indulgences manifest the genuinely communal dimension of Christian living: that the prayers of the saints can assist us in growth in holiness through purification and that our prayers can assist others in the same way. Though the root metaphor of a "treasury of merits" might seem inappropriately quantifying, the Catholic instinct that individual transformation in grace is bound up with communal living seems affirmed in this teaching about indulgences.

A presentation of the liturgical celebration of the sacrament concludes this section (1480-1484). While a Byzantine formula of absolution is quoted and the two communal forms of Roman rite celebration are noted, the CCC's cursory treatment of the liturgy of reconciliation is disappointing.

6.2. ANOINTING OF THE SICK (1499-1532)

Lumen gentium 11 provides the CCC's definition and description of the anointing of the sick:

> 1499 "By the sacred anointing of the sick and the prayer of the priests the whole church commends those who are ill to the suffering and glorified Lord, that he may raise them up and save them. And indeed she exhorts them to contribute to the good of the People of God by freely uniting themselves to the Passion and death of Christ."

Note that this sacrament not only allows those who are healthy to pray for the relief of suffering in those who are sick but also recognizes the mysterious role that the sick can play on behalf of the church and world by uniting their sufferings to those of Christ. In contrast to cultures that marginalize the sick, by means of this sacrament the church manifests its conviction that sick people have a special role to play in the life of the church and of the world:

> 1522 ...By celebrating this sacrament the Church, in the communion of saints, intercedes for the benefit of the sick person, and he, for his part, through the grace of this sacrament, contributes to the sanctification of the Church and to the good of all men for whom the Church suffers and offers herself through Christ to God the Father.

Remarking that sickness and suffering have always been among the most vexing problems marking human life, the CCC observes two fundamental human responses to the fact of sickness: illness can lead to preoccupation with the self or to a mature assessment of what is most essential in life, entailing a search for God or a return to God (1500-1501). The document sketches how sick people were viewed in the Old Testament, how Jesus's compassionate treatment of the sick confirmed his preaching of the kingdom of God, and how Christ commissioned the church to continue his mission of healing by taking up the cross, by the exercise of special healing charisms, by prayers of intercession, and by sacramental activity, especially the Eucharist and the anointing of the sick (1502-1510). The CCC then outlines the historical development of the sacrament of anointing:

> 1512 From ancient times in the liturgical traditions of both East and West, we have testimonies to the practice of anointings of the sick with blessed oil. Over the centuries the Anointing of the Sick was conferred more and more exclusively on those at the point of death. Because of this it received the name "Extreme Unction." Notwithstanding this evolution the liturgy has never failed to beg the Lord that the sick person may recover his health if it would be conducive to his salvation.

The Second Vatican Council called for the reform of the sacramental celebration of the anointing of the sick, and in 1972 the apostolic constitution *"Sacram unctionem infirmorum"* established the essential constituents of this sacrament for the Roman rite:

1513 ...

> The sacrament of the Anointing of the Sick is given
> to those who are seriously ill by anointing them on
> the forehead and hands with duly blessed oil—
> pressed from olives or from other plants—saying,
> only once: "Through this holy anointing may the
> Lord in his love and mercy help you with the grace
> of the Holy Spirit. May the Lord who frees you from
> sin save you and raise you up."

The recipients of this sacrament are not only those at the point of death; in fact, if one is in danger of death from illness or old age, one is certainly already a proper candidate for anointing. Unlike the Roman rite customs prior to Vatican II, the sacrament can be repeated during the course of an illness if the sick person's condition grows more grave. The sacrament can be conferred on those preparing for a serious operation or on the elderly who progressively become more frail. The CCC does not discuss certain pastoral initiatives that would extend the use of this sacrament to those suffering from emotional, psychological, or spiritual "illnesses," e.g., during recovery from alcohol or other drug addiction.

Basing its assertion on the teaching of the Council of Trent, the CCC states that only priests (i.e., presbyters and bishops) can serve as ministers of the anointing of the sick. James 5:14-15, with its reference to calling "for the elders (*presbyters*) of the church," has traditionally been seen as a scriptural warrant for restricting the ministers of this sacrament to priests. The CCC does not discuss requests being made to extend the administration of this sacrament to deacons and/or lay ministers who have direct connections with the care of the sick (e.g., hospital chaplains, pastoral visitors).

After a cursory sketch of the liturgical celebration of this sacrament (1517-1519), the CCC discusses four effects of receiving the sacrament. First, a particular grace of the Holy Spirit that strengthens people to overcome the difficulties associated with illness and/or old age is conferred in the sacrament. This strengthening heals the soul but may also heal the body if God so wills; forgiveness of sins is also associated with this gift of the Spirit. Second, the sick are consecrated to bear fruit by configuring themselves to the suffering Christ and by associating their sufferings with his saving passion. Third, the sick are confirmed in their ecclesial role as objects of the church's solicitude and witnesses to God's grace in the midst of suffering. Fourth, the sacrament may also prepare those on the point of death for their transition into eternal life, although the CCC makes it clear that viaticum (the technical term for the final eucharistic communion shared with a dying person) is the proper ritual prayer for the dying (1524-1525). The document makes a remarkable parallel between the sacraments of initiation and the sacraments of healing with viaticum:

> 1525 ...[J]ust as the sacraments of Baptism, Confirmation, and the Eucharist form a unity called "the sacraments of Christian initiation," so too it can be said that Penance, the Anointing of the Sick and the Eucharist as viaticum constitute at the end of Christian life "the sacraments that prepare for the heavenly homeland" or the sacraments that complete the earthly pilgrimage.

7.

THE SACRAMENTS OF SERVICE TO COMMUNION (1533-1666)

The final category of sacraments treated in the CCC is that of "sacraments in service to communion." In a few paragraphs the document attempts to draw theological links between the sacraments of holy orders and matrimony and the rest of the sacramental economy:

> 1533 Baptism, Confirmation and Eucharist are sacraments of Christian initiation. They ground the common vocation of all Christ's disciples, a vocation to holiness and to the mission of evangelizing the world. They confer the graces needed for the life according to the Spirit during this life as pilgrims on the march towards the homeland.

> 1534 Two other sacraments, Holy Orders and Matrimony, are directed towards the salvation of others; if they contribute as well to personal salvation, it is through service to others that they do so. They confer a particular mission in the Church and serve to build up the People of God.

> 1535 Through these sacraments those already *consecrated* by Baptism and Confirmation for the common priesthood of all the faithful can receive particular *consecrations*. Those who receive the sacrament of Holy Orders are *consecrated* in Christ's name "to feed the Church by the word and grace of God" [*Lumen gentium* 11 § 2]. On their part, "Christian spouses are fortified and, as it were, *consecrated* for the duties and dignity of their state by a special sacrament" [*Gaudium et spes* 48 § 2].

It should be recognized that the terminology and category of "sacraments of service to communion/to the community" is new in official Roman Catholic teaching. Such a designation and schema have some advantages. First, combatting a sacramental theology that concerned itself primarily with the "graces received" by the individual recipient, the CCC baldly states that those who receive holy orders or matrimony are transformed in holiness *insofar as* and *to the extent that* they spend themselves in service to others. This should challenge any attempt to present the ordained or those validly married as automatically in a "higher state" of holiness than others. Second, paralleling the consecrations received in ordination and in matrimony can raise some questions for pastoral practice: if one is called to ordination only after lengthy discernment and preparation for this way of life, should similar discernment and preparation mark those called to matrimony?

But there are also some disadvantages to this categorization. First, it can be argued (even on the basis of article 1533) that baptism and confirmation are the fundamental sacraments of service because all the baptized and confirmed accept a mission for the church and for the world as part of their call. Second, casual reading of the CCC could suggest that holy orders and matrimony are mutually exclusive consecrations, but in fact they are not: in addition to married deacons in the Roman rite, many Eastern Catholic rites recognize married presbyters, and married ministers of other denominations (after joining the Catholic communion and, in some cases, being ordained in the Roman rite) serve in holy orders. It would be more accurate to contrast matrimony with celibacy than with holy orders. Third, to designate holy orders and matrimony as particular specifications of the mission accepted in baptism and confirmation forces one to ask the question of the sacramental status of consecrated virgins, those in designated religious communities, and lay "professional" ministers. Are not these also specifications of the fundamental mission received in baptism and confirmation?

7.1. HOLY ORDERS (1536-1600)

Noting that the institution and mission of the apostolic ministry has already been treated in Part One (874-879), the CCC begins its discussion of holy orders as a sacrament of service to communion with a concise definition and description:

> 1536 Holy Orders is the sacrament through which the mission entrusted by Christ to his apostles continues to be exercised in the Church until the end of time: thus it is the sacrament of apostolic ministry. It includes three degrees: episcopate, presbyterate, and diaconate.

The document records that the terminology for this sacrament arose out of Roman civic usage in which *taxeis* or *ordines* indicated particular civil institutions, especially ones involved in government. Ancient ecclesiastical usage recognized orders of "overseers" (bishop), "elders" (presbyters), and "servants" (deacons) in addition to "catechumens," "virgins," "spouses" and "widows." (Some churches also recognized orders of "penitents" and of "the possessed" [*energoumenoi*].) "Ordination" was the act by which one was incorporated into a particular order, with an accompanying blessing. From this foundation the CCC describes present practice:

> 1538 ...Today the word "*ordination*" is reserved for the sacramental act which integrates a man into the order of bishops, presbyters, or deacons, and goes beyond a simple *election, designation, delegation,* or *institution* by the community, for it confers a gift of the Holy Spirit that permits the exercise of a "sacred power" (*sacra potestas*) which can only come from Christ himself through his Church. Ordination is also called *consecratio*, for it is a setting apart and an investiture by Christ himself for his Church....

Though this paragraph represents consistent official Roman Catholic teaching, it should also be noted that there is significant contemporary theological literature exploring how the "choice, designation, delegation, or institution" by the Christian community functioned as the concrete means by which the church determined God's conferral of "sacred power" on an individual through Christ in the power of the Holy Spirit.

Jesus himself was a Jewish layman, although some New Testament writings (especially the Letter to the Hebrews) present his life and deeds as the fulfillment of the Jewish priestly system.[1] Thus, after examining the Old Testament's prescriptions concerning special priestly groups within Israel; Christian liturgical prayers that bespeak a prefigurement of the New Testament ordained ministry in the priesthood of Aaron and his sons, the seventy elders, and the service of the Levites; and New Testament passages presenting Melchizedek as a prefigurement of Christ, the CCC strongly affirms the Christic foundation of all Christian ministry:

> 1545 The redemptive sacrifice of Christ is unique, accomplished once for all; yet it is made present in the Eucharistic sacrifice of the Church. The same is true of the one priesthood of Christ; it is made present through the ministerial priesthood without diminishing the uniqueness of Christ's priesthood: "Only Christ is the true priest, the others being only his ministers."

This heavy emphasis on the Christic foundation of all Christian ministry leads the CCC to describe two participations

---

[1] "Jesus was born a Jewish layman, conducted his ministry as a Jewish layman, and died a Jewish layman. There is no reliable historical tradition that he was of levitical or priestly descent....I have purposely emphasized Jesus' status as a layman because Christians are so accustomed to the imagery of Jesus the priest or the 'great high priest.' We owe this theological vision of Jesus the priest to a highly educated 1st-century Christian, otherwise unknown, who penned the NT Epistle to the Hebrews. Here, and here alone within the NT, Jesus is called a priest and a high priest" (John P. Meier, *A Marginal Jew: Rethinking the Historical Jesus*, vol. 1 of *The Roots of the Problem and the Person* (New York: Doubleday, 1991), 345, 348.

in the single priesthood of Christ: one belonging to the baptized as a whole, the other to the ministerial priesthood:

> 1547 The ministerial or hierarchical priesthood of bishops and priests, and the common priesthood of all the faithful participate, "each in its own proper way, in the one priesthood of Christ." While being "ordered one to another," they differ essentially. In what sense? While the common priesthood of the faithful is exercised by the unfolding of baptismal grace—a life of faith, hope, and charity, a life according to the Spirit—, the ministerial priesthood is at the service of the common priesthood. It is directed to the unfolding of the baptismal grace of all Christians. The ministerial priesthood is a *means* by which Christ unceasingly builds up and leads his Church....

As we have seen, the CCC presents the consecration received in the sacraments of initiation as foundational for participation in the church's mission. (Unfortunately the role of confirmation in equipping the baptized for such participation is neglected in the present article.) When one is consecrated by means of the sacrament of holy orders, one's participation in the church's mission is further specified, but the earlier baptismal consecration is not abrogated. Unlike contemporary distinctions between "clergy" and "laity," the vision enshrined here presents those ordained arising from and remaining a part of the *laos tou Theou* (the "People of God"), albeit with distinct status, tasks, and functions. There is no hint that ordination signals civic advancement or confers personal honor; ordination does not recognize extraordinary charisms or declare the recipient a saint. Rather, it confers a particular mission for the good of the church: the ministerial priesthood serves the common priesthood.[2] A major problem remains: how do

---

[2] Commenting on an earlier draft of this article, Peter Fink offers the following insightful analysis: "The Dogmatic Constitution on the Church" (*Lumen Gentium*) states: 'Though they differ essentially and not only in degree, the common priesthood of the faithful and

deacons fit into this framework? While defined as one of the "degrees" of holy orders, the diaconate is not part of the "ministerial or hierarchical priesthood" manifest in the episcopate and presbyterate. As ordained ministers, deacons serve the common priesthood of the baptized (and confirmed), yet they do not participate in the ministerial priesthood as presbyters and bishops do.

All ordained ministers share a dual representative function: acting *in persona Christi Capitis* ("in the person of Christ as head [of the church]"), they iconically manifest Christ to the church and world; acting *in nomine ecclesiae* ("in the name of the church"), they iconically represent the church before God. But as the following citations witness, the role of the deacon in these two functions remains obscure:

> 1548 In the ecclesial service of the ordained minister, it is Christ himself who is present to his Church as Head of his Body, Shepherd of his flock, high priest of the

---

the ministerial or hierarchical priesthood are nonetheless ordered to one another; each in its own proper way shares in the one priesthood of Christ' (no. 10). The catechism makes the subordinate phrase primary: 'The priesthood of bishops and of priests differs essentially from that of the faithful, although they are "ordered to one another; each in its proper way shares in the one priesthood of Christ."'....*Lumen Gentium* gives priority to the relationship and mutual ordering; the catechism gives priority to the difference....

"This stress on the uniqueness of the ordained priesthood is important. The stress on the relationship between the two modes of Christ's priesthood, however, is equally important. The language of Vatican II was clearly designed to counter centuries of neglect of the priesthood of the baptized and to establish this priesthood in relationship to the ordained priest. The truth of the matter is that neither the difference nor the relationship is subordinate to the other. There is a difference of degree and kind between the two, and at the same time a relationship and mutual ordering between them" (Peter E. Fink, "The Liturgy and Eucharist in the Catechism," in *The Universal Catechism Reader: Reflections and Responses*, ed. Thomas J. Reese (San Francisco: HarperSanFrancisco, 1990), 103-104.

redemptive sacrifice, Teacher of Truth. This is what the church means by saying that the priest, in virtue of the sacrament of Holy Orders, acts *in persona Christi Capitis*....

1552 The ministerial priesthood has the task not only of representing Christ—Head of the Church—before the assembly of the faithful, but also of acting in the name of the whole Church when presenting to God the prayer of the Church, and above all when offering the Eucharistic sacrifice.

The CCC's treatment of the three "degrees" of the sacrament of holy orders sketches how each fulfills the pastoral office with its *munera* of authoritative proclamation of God's Word, presidency at the church's worship, and oversight of the church's life. Episcopal ordination confers the "fullness" of the sacrament of holy orders, enabling a bishop to represent Christ and act in his name in teaching, sanctifying, and governing in collegial connection with other bishops throughout the world (1555-1561). Presbyteral ordination confers this ability to represent Christ and act in his name to a lesser degree than bishops; presbyters, whether secular or religious, are called to be "co-workers" with the episcopal order in teaching, sanctifying, and governing (1562-1568). Diaconal ordination likewise empowers a person to represent Christ and act in his name, but not as a member of the ministerial priesthood; deacons are configured to Christ the servant ("deacon") as they assist bishops and presbyters in teaching, sanctifying, and governing (1569-1571).

Following the teaching of Pius XII in his 1947 apostolic constitution *Sacramentum Ordinis*, the CCC designates the "matter" and "form" of the sacrament of Holy Orders as follows:

1573 The *essential rite* of the sacrament of Holy Orders for all three degrees consists in the bishop's imposition of hands on the head of the ordinand and in the bishop's specific consecratory prayer asking God for the outpouring of the Holy Spirit and his gifts proper to the ministry to which the candidate is being ordained.

Unfortunately the document's exploration of the liturgical celebration of the sacrament is quite meager, probably because the ceremonies are quite diverse in the various Eastern and Western liturgical traditions. (Roman rite readers should be aware that a major revision of the 1968 ordination rites was promulgated in 1990, although its official English translation has not yet been approved for the dioceses of the United States.[3])

The CCC teaches that validly ordained bishops validly confer the three degrees of holy orders and that only baptized males can validly receive the sacrament. Citing John Paul II's *Mulieris dignitatem* 26-27 and the 1976 declaration of the Congregation for the Doctrine of the Faith *Inter insigniores* on the admission of women to the priesthood, the CCC offers a single argument for excluding women as proper subjects of ordination: the intention of Christ:

> 1577 "Only a baptized man (*vir*) validly receives sacred ordination" [*Code of Canon Law* 1024]. The Lord Jesus chose men (*viri*) to form the college of the twelve apostles, and the apostles did the same when they chose collaborators to succeed them in their ministry. The college of bishops, with whom the priests are united in the priesthood, makes the college of the twelve an

---

3 For further information on the 1990 ordination rites, see J. M. Joncas, "The New Roman Rite Prayer of Ordination of Presbyters: A Liturgical Vision of the Priesthood, *The Priest* 48, no. 5 (May 1992): 39-47; idem, "Naming the Tasks of Presbyteral Ministry: A Comparison of the *Promissio Electorum* in the 1968 and 1990 Roman Rite Ordination Ritual," in *In Service of the Church: Essays on Theology and Ministry Honoring Reverend Charles L. Froehle*, ed. Victor J. Klimoski and Mary Christine Athans (St. Paul, Minnesota: St. Paul Seminary School of Divinity University of St. Thomas, 1993), 101-116; idem, "The Public Language of Ministry Revisited: *De Ordinatione Episcopi, Presbyterorum et Diaconorum* 1990," *Worship* 68, no. 5 (1994): 386-403.

> ever-present and ever-active reality until Christ's return.
> The Church recognizes herself to be bound by this choice
> made by the Lord himself. For this reason the ordination
> of women is not possible.

This article is misleading. First, exegetes distinguish between "the Twelve" and "apostles" because, for example, Paul presents himself as an apostle without being a member of the Twelve. "Apostolic succession" and "collegial representation of the Twelve" are thus not synonymous: the way in which the college of bishops succeeds to the mission of the college of the Twelve needs to be very carefully nuanced. Second, the statement that "ordination of women is not possible" strictly applies only to the ordination of women to the priesthood (i.e., the presbyterate and/or the episcopate). Ordination of women to the diaconate is not only possible, but there is evidence that ancient churches did so (cf. the *Testamentum Domini* and the *Apostolic Constitutions*). However, in the light of John Paul II's recent request not to continue discussion on the ordination of women to the priesthood, I will refrain from commenting on the difficulties involved in determining the intention of Jesus vis-à-vis the establishment of a three-degreed ordained ministry and the genders of those to serve in this ministry.

Articles 1579-1580 outline the different disciplinary patterns of Eastern and Western churches connecting celibacy and the ordained ministry. In the West deacons may be married or celibate, while presbyters and bishops are chosen from the ranks of celibates; in the East deacons and presbyters may be celibate or married, while bishops are chosen from the ranks of celibates. The CCC notes that both traditions prescribe that once one has received the sacrament of holy orders one cannot marry. Catechists should be aware that pastoral initiatives are questioning this prescription (e.g., should a married deacon whose wife has died leaving him with children to raise be prevented from remarrying for the sake of his family's welfare?).

The CCC concludes its treatment of the sacrament of holy orders by considering its effects: an indelible spiritual mark (*character*) signifying that once validly ordained a person cannot be re-ordained (1581-1584) and the grace of the Holy Spirit equipping the minister for his activity in the church (1585-1588).

7.2. MATRIMONY (1601-1666)

Canon 1055/1, citing *Gaudium et spes* 48/1, provides the CCC with its definition of matrimony:

> 1601 "The matrimonial covenant, by which a man and a woman establish between themselves a partnership of the whole of life, is by its nature ordered toward the good of the spouses and the procreation and education of offspring; this covenant between baptized persons has been raised by Christ the Lord to the dignity of a sacrament" [*Code of Canon Law* 1055 § 1].

The CCC examines the evolution of this institution from marriage to matrimony under four headings: marriage "in the order of creation," "under the regime of sin," "under the pedagogy of the Law," and "in the Lord." The first heading is needed to account theologically for the fact that marriage existed long before the time of Jesus, the Mosaic covenant, or the Jewish patriarchs and that it also exists today among non-Christians and those who profess no religion:

> 1603 ...The vocation to marriage is written in the very nature of man and woman as they came from the hand of the Creator. Marriage is not a purely human institution despite the many variations it may have undergone through the centuries in different cultures, social structures, and spiritual attitudes. These differences should not cause us to forget its common and permanent characteristics. Although the dignity of this institution is not transparent everywhere with the same clarity, some sense

of the greatness of the matrimonial union exists in all cultures....

The assertions in this paragraph need to be confronted with historical and anthropological studies on the institution of marriage.

The second heading reflects Catholic teaching on nature and grace: the institution of marriage, founded in the order of creation for humankind's good, has been derailed by sin (like other human institutions), yet it has not been utterly destroyed. With God's grace, what was intended by God for humankind in the order of creation can be restored in the order of redemption:

> 1606 Every man experiences evil around him and within himself. This experience makes itself felt in the relationships between man and woman. Their union has always been threatened by discord, a spirit of domination, infidelity, jealousy, and conflicts that can escalate into hatred and separation. This disorder can manifest itself more or less acutely, and can be more or less overcome according to the circumstances of cultures, eras, and individuals, but it does seem to have a universal character.

> 1607 According to faith the disorder we notice so painfully does not stem from the *nature* of man and woman, nor from the nature of their relations, but from *sin*. As a break with God, the first sin had for its first consequence the rupture of the original communion between man and woman. Their relations were distorted by mutual recriminations; their mutual attraction, the Creator's own gift, changed into a relationship of domination and lust; and the beautiful vocation of man and woman to be fruitful, multiply, and subdue the earth was burdened by the pain of childbirth and the toil of work.

> 1608 Nevertheless, the order of creation persists, though seriously disturbed. To heal the wounds of sin, man and woman need the help of the grace that God in his infinite

mercy never refuses them. Without his help man and woman cannot achieve the union of their lives for which God created them "in the beginning."

The third heading acknowledges that both the institution of marriage itself and theological reflection upon it developed in ancient Israel. The patriarchs and monarchs of Israel practiced polygamy; only gradually did a monogamous understanding of marriage come to the fore, as witnessed in prophetic literature such as Hosea, in the edifying tales of the books of Ruth and Tobit, and in the poetry of the Song of Songs.

The final heading treats specifically Christian marriage, founded in the preaching and teaching of Jesus himself on the covenantal and permanent character of matrimony:

> 1615 This unequivocal insistence on the indissolubility of the marriage bond may have left some perplexed and could seem to be a demand impossible to realize. However, Jesus has not placed on spouses a burden impossible to bear, or too heavy—heavier than the Law of Moses. By coming to restore the original order of creation disturbed by sin, he himself gives the strength and grace to live marriage in the new dimension of the Reign of God. It is by following Christ, renouncing themselves, and taking up their crosses that spouses will be able to "receive" the original meaning of marriage and live it with the help of Christ. This grace of Christian marriage is a fruit of Christ's cross, the source of all Christian life.

In the context of the Christic character of matrimony, the CCC inserts a few articles on virginity for the sake of the reign of God (1618-1620). Both matrimony and consecrated virginity are presented as responses to the grace of Christ, specifications of baptismal grace and of equal status in the life of the church. The document does not assert that virginity (or celibacy, for that matter) is a "higher calling" than matrimony, but sees them as mutually reinforcing:

1620 Both the sacrament of Matrimony and virginity for the Kingdom of God come from the Lord himself. It is he who gives them meaning and grants them the grace which is indispensable for living them out in conformity with his will. Esteem of virginity for the sake of the kingdom and the Christian understanding of marriage are inseparable, and they reinforce each other....

The CCC notes differences between the Eastern and Western liturgical traditions of celebrating matrimony that affect theological understanding of the ministers and recipients of the sacrament:

1623 In the Latin church, it is ordinarily understood that the spouses, as ministers of Christ's grace, mutually confer upon each other the sacrament of Matrimony by expressing their consent before the Church. In the Eastern liturgies the minister of this sacrament (which is called "Crowning") is the priest or bishop who, after receiving the mutual consent of the spouses, successively crowns the bridegroom and the bride as a sign of the marriage covenant.

This leads to a discussion of the character of Christian matrimonial consent, the conditions required to bestow it, the role of priest or deacon and witnesses in observing the exchange of consent during the liturgy of marriage, and the nature of marriages contracted between a Roman Catholic Christian and a baptized Christian of another denomination ("mixed marriage") or between a Roman Catholic Christian and a non-baptized person ("disparity of cult" [1625-1637]). For completeness' sake, the CCC should also have mentioned marriages involving catechumens, which fall into a special category.

The CCC teaches that there are two principal effects of receiving the sacrament of matrimony. First, the covenant pledged between the spouses establishes a permanent marriage bond (1639-1640). Second, the spouses receive a grace proper to the sacrament to perfect their love for one another, to strengthen their unity, and to equip them for raising and educating children (1641-1642).

The document further teaches that there are three principal goods with corresponding requirements arising from conjugal love. First, the good of marital unity forbids polygamous marriages or concubinage, even in cultures where these are legally acceptable (1644-1645). Second, the good of marital fidelity exhorts spouses to unshakable unity:

> 1648 It can seem difficult, even impossible, to bind oneself for life to another human being. This makes it all the more important to proclaim the Good News that God loves us with a definitive and irrevocable love, that married couples share in this love, that it supports them and sustains them, and that by their own faithfulness they can be witnesses to God's faithful love. Spouses who with God's grace give this witness, often in very difficult conditions, deserve the gratitude and support of the ecclesial community.

The CCC recognizes, however, that there may be situations in which separation of the spouses is permissible or even necessary as long as no new matrimonial covenant is attempted with another human being (1649). The CCC further teaches that those who have civilly divorced from their matrimonial partner and contracted another civil marriage before the death of the former spouse and without a declaration of nullity on the part of the church incur certain penalties:

> 1650 Today there are numerous Catholics in many countries who have recourse to civil *divorce* and contract new civil unions. In fidelity to the words of Jesus Christ— "Whoever divorces his wife and marries another, commits adultery against her; and if she divorces her husband and marries another, she commits adultery" [Mk 10:11-12]—the Church maintains that a new union cannot be recognized as valid, if the first marriage was. If the divorced are remarried civilly, they find themselves in a situation that objectively contravenes God's law. Consequently, they cannot receive Eucharistic communion as

long as this situation persists. For the same reason, they cannot exercise certain ecclesial responsibilities. Reconciliation through the sacrament of Penance can be granted only to those who have repented for having violated the sign of the covenant and of fidelity to Christ, and who are committed to living in complete continence.

The document does not refer to the so-called "internal forum" or "good conscience" approaches to the admission of such Catholics to communion. Third, the good of openness to fertility demands that Christian spouses "accept children lovingly from God" and pledge themselves to develop their physical, mental, moral, spiritual, and supernatural life (1652-1654).

The CCC concludes its teaching on the sacrament of matrimony with a few reflections on the "domestic church" (1655-1657) and a statement on single people in the church and world (1658). The latter is especially disappointing in its cursory treatment of a significant proportion of present-day Catholics.

8.

OTHER CELEBRATIONS (1667-1690)

The CCC discusses certain communal prayer practices beyond the seven sacraments in its final articles in Part Two: sacramentals (1667-1673), popular devotions (1674-1676) and Christian funeral rites (1680-1690).

Quoting the teaching of SC 60, the document defines sacramentals as sacred signs signifying effects obtained through the intercession of the church. Unlike sacraments functioning *ex opere operato*, the sacramentals achieve their effects *ex opere operantis*, preparing believers to receive sacramental grace and to cooperate with it. Blessings constitute the primary category of sacramentals; these blessings may be of persons (e.g., abbots, abbesses, virgins, those professing membership in a religious community, readers, acolytes, catechists, etc.), of human activities (e.g., meals, going to and rising from sleep, etc.), of objects (e.g., altars, holy oils, sacred vessels, vestments, bells, etc.), or of places (e.g., churches, oratories, shrines, etc.). Exorcisms comprise a secondary category of sacramentals; these ritual prayers invoke the power of God to free people from demonic influence or possession. The CCC clearly distinguishes possession from mental illness.

The document's treatment of popular devotions is quite sketchy. Noting that the religious instincts of various peoples have found outlets in extra-sacramental activities such as veneration of relics, visits to shrines, pilgrimages, processions, stations of the cross, religious dance, the praying of the rosary, and the wearing of medals, the CCC cautions that such devotions must extend the sacramental life of the church, not replace it. Evaluation and possible "purification" of popular devotions is remanded to the judgment of bishops and the general norms of the church.

Finally, the CCC presents the stational character of Christian funeral rites, all expressing the paschal character of

Christian death. Rites in the home (or funeral home in many parts of the United States) allow the Christian community to console the family and friends of the deceased with a word of faith. In the church building, a Liturgy of the Word helps the community to grapple with the mystery of death and resurrection in the light of the church's heritage; the eucharistic liturgy actualizes what is proclaimed in the Liturgy of the Word. The commendation, celebrated in the church or at graveside, allows the community to bid a final farewell to the deceased in the sure hope of meeting again in Christ.

CONCLUSION

My few reflections on the sacramental life of Roman Catholic Christians can be crowned with the inspiring words of a twentieth-century Orthodox theologian. Alexander Schmemann evokes the beauty and power of the sacramental life at the conclusion of his essay "And Ye Are Witnesses of These Things"[1]:

> The Church is the sacrament of the Kingdom—not because she possesses divinely instituted acts called "sacraments," but because first of all she is the possibility given to man to see in and through this world the "world to come," to see and to "live" it in Christ. It is only when in the darkness of *this world* we discern that Christ has *already* "filled all things with Himself" that these *things*, whatever they may be, are revealed and given to us full of meaning and beauty. A Christian is the one who, wherever he looks, finds Christ and rejoices in Him. And this joy *transforms* all his human plans and programs, decisions and actions, making all his mission the sacrament of the world's return to Him who is the life of the world.

---

[1] In *For the Life of the World: Sacraments and Orthodoxy* (New York: St. Vladimir's Seminary Press, 1973), 113.